Successful Home Schooling

by

J. Richard Fugate

Aletheia Division of Alpha Omega Publications
Tempe, Arizona

TABLE OF CONTENTS

Introduction

This booklet is designed for parents who are just considering home schooling as well as those who are already in their first year. It should be read two or three times before and during the first year as more will be comprehended after reaching different experience levels in home schooling.

The various sections of this booklet have been compiled from articles I have written for home school publications and from speeches presented to home school conventions. The content of these articles and speeches was developed to help parents understand the reasons behind home schooling and its importance to children and parents.

Since the material is basic, it can be very helpful in answering the questions of family and friends who are confused and even intimidated by those of you who are already home schooling. Some of these people may wonder why the public schools they believe are good enough for their children, aren't good enough for yours. Relatives particularly may be concerned that your children will be shorted on their education or socialization. If you find this booklet does not contain all of the information you need to handle these or any other issues, let me know so that it can be expanded to include that information for others.

I hope this material is an encouragement. You really can do it! You, as hundreds of thousands of other parents today, are able to teach your own children. In fact, studies have shown that you are likely to provide your children with a much more superior education than they could receive by any other means. This fact is in addition to your protecting them from definite dangers which could destroy their souls. May God also encourage you and grant you understanding as you study the enclosed information.

SECTION I

ISSUES TO CONSIDER

This section addresses the most common concerns thinking people have about home schooling. It covers the reasons Christian parents need to protect their children from negative peer pressure and humanistic teachings. Then, it suggests how to prevent having legal problems with state or local officials. This section also provides information on how home school children receive positive socialization and how even parents greatly benefit from home schooling. These articles should arm you with the answers you need, make you more secure in your decision to home school, and also help set at ease those who are concerned about your new endeavor.

So, You Want to Home School Your Child?

If you are new to home schooling, you are probably overwhelmed with the apparent complexities of the whole issue. Gone are the days when my wife and I withdrew our three children from their schools, bought the only curriculum we knew of, ignored our limitations, and began to teach them at home. All we knew was that they weren't staying any longer in the public and Christian schools they were attending. We were convicted not to leave them where humanism was being taught and where they were surrounded with peers who negatively influenced them away from God's Word. For us it was simple, plenty of conviction, followed by the only logical action available.

Today the situation is much more complex. There are tens of curriculum choices available and at least two conflicting philosophies on when to start teaching your child. Also, there are a multiplicity of opinions by veteran home schoolers on exactly how it should be done. All of this adds up to a confusing maze for the starting home schooler. Because of these factors, I believe many potential home school families are scared off for the wrong reasons.

In my opinion, there are only three main things that determine success or failure for home schoolers.

1. Personal conviction about the right philosophical reason for home schooling (i.e. the fact that God holds parents alone accountable for their children's soul training and that training in most schools is humanistic and/or forces relationships with ungodly peer influence). Without this conviction many home school families place (or return) their children in public schools after a couple of years of home schooling.

2. Proper family government where the father recognizes the importance of, is in favor of, and is the leader in the decision of home schooling. Home schooling is hampered in most families where the mother trys to carry the task single handedly.

Sometimes the marriage can even be damaged when the father is not in favor of her going ahead without his leadership.

3. Parents who are committed to train up their children as unto the Lord and who are willing to follow God's Word to achieve these goals.

It is this last point that is crucial to your success. Your educational background is not important (you can learn along with the kids), nor is your lack of experience (you have taught your children for years), but your ability to cause your children to obey is essential. While lack of personal conviction may lead to many parents quitting; and mothers home schooling without at least the father's support will diminish the success of home schooling; not learning how to control your children will most likely cause complete failure.

Helping you with this crucial issue of causing your children to obey is covered in depth by my book, *What the Bible Says About ...Child Training*. Many parents have told me it has made the difference between failure and success for them. To God be the glory.

Let's summarize some key factors about Biblical child training as it directly relates to home schooling.

• Every child has a human nature which is self-centered and which must be restrained by his parents (Psalms 51:5; 58:3; Proverbs 29:15; I Samuel 3:13; Romans 5:12,14). This nature will interfere with effective home schooling through laziness, rebellion, or willfullness. Parents will need to identify these negative character traits and then to control them by the proper use of their authority.

• There are two facets of child training, controlling and teaching. As any successful teacher can tell you, you cannot teach children who are not under control. Obviously, parents will need to exert their authority with children who are not yet trained: to hold still and listen during instruction, to not

3

disrupt others, to concentrate and apply themselves to their work, to strive for excellence, etc.

- The control facet of child training is the most difficult for the parent because it means facing conflict, using your authority, and overcoming the weakness of your own nature. However, it is also a most rewarding facet because it is here that you can see a child released from his or her personal character weaknesses and begin to develop into a mature individual.

- The teaching facet of child training is really the easiest part. A child who is under control can be taught anything, from any curriculum, with any method. The parent is, of course, responsible to see that the content of the teaching is in line with God's truth.

Sadly, there are some parents who cannot easily home school their children. Single parents obviously must work, mothers and fathers with unwilling mates, and families in which both parents truly **must** work may be unable to teach their own children. However, even these families can supply home schooling for their children in many cases. Another home schooling family could teach one or more of your children. This solution can be beneficial for both families as true Christian giving and receiving is practiced. Local support groups are good places to find such an arrangement

May I encourage you to try home schooling if you have the personal conviction, the proper family government, and a true commitment to God for your children's training. I promise that opportunity for soul and spiritual growth will be enormous for the entire family. If you persevere through the tests, the rewards will be great. Even if you only home school for a year, it can be the single most important year in your lives. May God richly bless your endeavor.

Whose Responsibility is Christian Education?

Children are entrusted to parents by God (Psalm 127:3). They belong to God and He has given them into our care, thus creating specific stewardship responsibilities. God has a plan and purpose for each child. Each child is a life from God that is placed in a specific family as a part of that plan. God has set children under their parents' control for approximately one-third of their lives. Unlike animals that raise their young for only a few months, children are dependent on their parents for an extensive training period. Animals need to receive training only for physical existence, but a child requires training for his soul. Parents are responsible to train their children according to God's standards. It is, therefore, the primary duty of parents to guide their children's lives for the purposes of God, and to train them as He would have them trained (Deuteronomy 4:9; 6:7; Psalm 78:3-6; Proverbs 6:20-23; 13:1; 22:6; Ephesians 6:4).

Many Christian parents understand that it is impossible to "... train up a child in the way he should go ..." and at the same time turn him over to a humanistic, secularized, government education. We are told that children are not "... to hear instruction that causeth to err from the words of knowledge" (Proverbs 19:27). Obviously, public schools are not much of an option for Christian parents. Even many Christian schools have become worldly in their attempt to compare favorably with the public schools. They have admitted non-Christian children from non-Christian families thus lowering their standards; and some have even excluded students who are below grade level in order to keep the school's academic record high and thus impress the world. Therefore, Christian parents are increasingly choosing home schooling as an alternative to public or even private education.

But, you say, how can I teach my own child? You have already been teaching your child from birth to this very day. Who taught him to walk, talk, eat, dress, wash, count, read, tell time, distinguish colors, and a hundred other lessons? Is this all you know or don't you also know parts of speech, fractions, and at least twelve years of other information (especially when you can bone up on each lesson ahead of your child). You not only *can* teach your own child, you will likely do a better job than any school can do — and that is a proven fact. More importantly, you can protect your child from the dangers he would definitely encounter in public school and also train him consistently in God's way. These two things are commanded by God's Word, while academic education is not. It is easy to see which God considers most important.

Of course, every young person needs to be prepared for adulthood and an academic education is a part of that preparation. Every Christian parent should determine that their child will receive the best academic preparation possible so that Christians can give a testimony of excellence in any profession. Certainly, Amercia's schools have proven themselves to be a dismal failure in providing quality academic education over the last 20 years. Total expenses, teachers' pay, added administrators, teachers' education, have all increased greatly while SAT scores have dropped drastically. (Schools of Choice, U.S. Senate Republican Policy Committee Report. Aug. 1989.) Home schooling allows the best educational methodology – tutoring – to be utilized in the best environment possible, the home. Try it, you'll love it.

Not every family can home school. Single parents and mothers who **must** work obviously are blocked, as are mothers whose husbands are against her staying home and teaching. Some parents are simply too immature to sacrifice personal desires for their children (i.e. possessions, careers, or even their time). A few mothers have said they are just too disorganized or scatterbrained to conduct a home school. I believe that even these mothers and their children would benefit from home schooling, which could improve their problems through practical experience.

Should Your Child Ever Go to Public School?

Part I

The ever-growing home school movement has encouraged me to think there is still hope for our nation. Every parent who has taken the giant step of removing his children from public education should be commended for doing a good work.

However, a huge black cloud is appearing on the horizon that threatens the home school movement even more than government intervention. This ominous threat is the lack of understanding among many home schoolers concerning the really important reasons for keeping their children out of the public schools. Therefore, approximately 50 percent of former home schooled children are now being returned to the public system each year.

I was naive enough to think that because families went into home schooling in the first place that they understood the real danger of public education. Therefore, I never dreamed that they would be willing to return their children to the public school under any circumstances. Obviously, some parents may consider returning their children to public school due to economics, but even they need to understand first the danger awaiting their family.

The most serious danger in sending your child to public school, in my opinion, is detrimental peer influence. Peer influence teaches a child that right and wrong are based on what is or is not acceptable to the peer group. Your child's classmates, playmates, and even most of his friends will not have been taught the same standards of behavior or thinking that your child has been taught. Right and wrong for these children is what they have learned from TV and accepted from their peers. If your child attempts to uphold the standards you have taught him, these children will make him feel that he is strange, weird, and an outcast.

As adults, we are far less vulnerable to peer pressure than children who can be crushed by their worldly peers. We tend to forget how much we were influenced by peers in our youth.

The average child is quickly conditioned to not oppose the views of the crowd. He then gradually begins to embrace the standards of his peers in his desire for *social acceptance*. He thus becomes alienated from his parents and even resents them. Eventually, the majority of children will accept those very standards which disagree with their parents' standards.

The potential danger of peer pressure to your children is reason enough for you to isolate them from its evil influence. Even the Christian school may not be the answer. Unfortunately, many Christian schools are just businesses, with Christian employees, struggling to grow big enough to exist. Therefore, they often accept children who have no training, from families with no standards, thereby resulting in the same negative peer pressure which exists in the public system.

I don't understand how parents can subject their children to this insidious threat which claims so many. I am weary of hearing from parents whose teens have turned away from them and their values, and aligned themselves with their peers and the world's thinking. Are you willing to take that chance with your child's soul? Before you do, please talk to some of the older parents who have lost their children to the world system and are honest enough to tell you why.

Children are not soldiers to be thrown into battle unarmed and untrained against an enemy they do not know. They are little ones to be protected from harm (Matthew 18:6). Please, do not let your little ones be destroyed or injured in the spiritual warfare before they are prepared. "... bad company corrupts good morals ..." (I Corinthians 15:33). "He who walks with wise men will be wise, but the companion of fools will suffer harm." (Proverbs 13:20).

Should Your Child Ever Go to Public School?
Part II

In the last section I suggested that the peer influence your child would face in a public school, or even in an open enrollment Christian school, is the number one danger to his soul. However, a more subtle, but equally insidious, threat to your child is the philosophy that he will be taught through secular education. That philosophy is humanism, and it rests on the belief that there is no God and, therefore, man is his own god.

I don't believe that Christian parents would send their child to a school run by Buddhists or Hindus to study a curriculum written by their dedicated leaders under teachers trained to question their students' values and to replace them with their own. However, the secular educational system in America today is exactly that – a religion with its own moral code, its own instruction manuals, and many dedicated followers to teach your child the religion of humanism.

Secular textbooks are the tip of an iceberg which must be intensively analyzed. Teacher editions are more bold, and give direction to the teacher that, when followed, will result in the tearing down of traditional Biblical values in the minds and souls of most students. The values specifically attacked are: the proper parent/child relationships, male and female roles as ordained by God, moral absolutes and human accountability to them, nationalism, and finally, the very existence of God.

The base of the iceberg is the teacher's training in colleges and on-going seminars which are influenced by the NEA. This training impresses the teacher with the need to replace the traditional value system that many parents have taught their children with the "superior" values of humanism. Of course, most teachers are unwitting agents to this objective. They merely concentrate on the technical aspects of teaching and don't analyze the content or understand the issue of humanism. But you need to understand this issue. In fact, you owe it to your children to protect them from it.

Listen to what some of the humanist leaders have openly said about their intentions:

John Dewey, dedicated humanist, the father of U.S. progressive education, and once the head of Columbia University's Teachers College stated: **"There is no God and there is no soul ... There is no room for fixed, natural law or moral absolutes."**

Over fifty years ago Charles Francis Potter, a signer of *Humanist Manifesto I*, wrote in his book, *Humanism, A New Religion*: *"Education is thus a most powerful ally of humanism, and every public school is a school of humanism. What can the theistic Sunday schools, meeting for an hour once a week, and teaching only a fraction of the children, do to stem the tide of a five-day program of humanistic teaching?"* (p. 128).

And to confirm that the humanists are today perhaps even more militant, John Dunphy wrote in the January/February, 1983, issue of the *Humanist Magazine*: *"I am convinced the battle for human-kind's future must be waged and won in the public school classroom by teachers who correctly perceive their role as the proselytizer of a new faith: a religion of humanity that recognizes and respects what theologians call divinity in every human being.*

*"The classroom must and will become an arena of conflict between the old and the new – the rotting corpse of Christianity together with all its adjacent evils and misery, and the new faith of humanism ...but humanism will emerge triumphant. It **must** if the family of humankind is to survive."*

Is this the kind of person you want to control your child's thinking? Before you consider sending your child to a public school, study the issues for yourself by reading one or more of the excellent books on humanism such as Tim LaHaye's, *The Battle for The Mind*; Mel & Norma Gabler's, *What Are They Teaching Our Children?*; or *Child Abuse in the Classroom*, edited by Phyllis Schlaffly. Your child's well-being in life, in fact his very soul, may depend on your decision.

The Socialization Issue

But how will my children learn to get along well with others their own age if they miss out on the group activities at a school? This concern does not arise from any research proving that peer contact in childhood produces positive socialization. In fact, research proves that 89% of home school children actually test at or above the national average of regularly schooled children in the area of social development.

"Some critics of home schooling argue that students educated at home are deprived socially. However, Dr. Taylor [chairman of the department of education at Heartland College] found that the Piers-Harris Children's Self-Concept Scale, one of the best self-concept instruments available, proves otherwise. The Scale was used to evaluate 224 randomly selected home schooling participants in grades four through twelve. One half of the participants scored above the 90th percentile on the scale, and only 10.3 percent scored below the national average (Taylor, J.W. Self-Concept in Home-Schooling Children. Ann Arbor, MI: University of Michigan, 1986)." *The Home School Court Report*, March-June, 1987.

The emotional concerns many parents feel (that their little one may not learn to relate well to others — to have friends, to avoid ridicule, etc.) may come from the pain they remember from their own negative social experiences. Parents should ask themselves if they ever learned a healthy self-concept by being exposed to childhood peers. Usually only the extroverts, bullies, clowns, and popular thrive in this atmosphere. Many sensitive children are damaged for life.

It *has* been proven that children who spend a high percentage of their time with peers rather than adults become peer-dependent and soon begin to question, then reject, parental authority. The fact that one half of the children in the Piers-Harris test mentioned above scored in the *top ten percent* proves what an increasing number of psychologists and even sociologists are beginning to say that children, especially young children, would be far better remaining at home with their parents than being thrown into peer groups to fend for themselves.

Children relate to those with whom they have the most contact. If that contact is with children, they will relate most with children. If it is with adults, they will relate most with adults. Children, as undeveloped little people, need acceptable, mature models to imitate, not their undeveloped, immature, or even distorted peers.

A teenager will follow the leadership of whomever becomes his authority. This **should** be the parents, but if they have allowed the child to develop heros from TV or movie actors, video music stars, neighborhood or school kids, then those heros will be the child's major influence. This type of allegiance is extremely difficult to break due to the tight bond of social dependency that develops between commrades. It is not unlike the problem the alcoholic or drug addict has over his friends which he must give up along with his addiction.

Some Christian parents honestly believe that their children **should** be left in the world as a Biblical issue. These parents have been influenced by the philosophy of existential humanists who believe we each should experience everything as the only way of knowing. Their philosophy says that a child should not be placed in a greenhouse and so protected from the world's dangers by which he is supposedly toughened and matured. As with most existentialist positions, logic reveals its false conclusions. The very idea of a greenhouse is to totally protect a young, weak, easily-damaged sapling from disease, hostile elements, and destruction. Only after the young plant is sufficiently matured to the point its guardian is **sure** it is ready to brave the elements on its own, does he replant the healthy and strong plant in the outside world. To throw young, untrained children into the world to be "lights of the world" before the eyes of their souls have even opened, is throwing these children into Satan's hands to confuse or even to destroy.

It's like Dr. Roy Lowrie, former headmaster of Delaware County Christian School and author of *The Christian School*, said (paraphrased): It is really the students in the public school who are sheltered from the real world. They are sheltered from knowing God the Creator, the Provider, and the Savior. They are prevented from learning about fallen man and Satan. They are sheltered from learning the absolute truth of moral laws meant for man's protection from evil. Finally, they are sheltered from the Word of God, and its life changing effect on each of them personally.

The following two articles further explain this subject more completely and are reprinted here by permission from the authors and from:

> *The Teaching Home*
> P.O. Box 20219
> Portland, OR 97220-0219

Problem and Cause of Peer Dependency Revealed
by Gregg Harris, Director, *Christian Life Workshops*

Social psychologists and educators have been warning us for more than a decade that a social phenomenon called "age-segregated, peer-group dependency" is becoming a national problem among children as young as 5 and 6 years old.

Dr. Urie Bronfenbrenner, Professor of Child Development and Family Studies at Cornell University, cautioned in 1970 that a "vacuum, moral and emotional" created by the negligence of the family, the church, and the public school is being filled by television and "the socially-isolated, age-graded peer group." According to Bronfenbrenner, if society continues to remove parents, other adults, and older children from active participation in the lives of children, we can expect "alienation, indifference, antagonism, and violence on the part of the younger generation."

Peer dependency is a very real problem.

Dr. Albert Bandura, at Stanford University, reports signs that age-peer dependency is moving down into the preschool levels as more families turn to earlier and earlier out-of-home child care. What used to pass as adolescent rebellion is now being observed on the preschool level as well. Some researchers are suggesting that some adolescent rebellion may, in fact, be an acute case of peer dependency "coming out of the closet." When the child finally develops the physical prowess and confidence to express his disdain for adult norms, he begins to do so.

These researchers and educators have been warning us for years that the modern child is often isolated from the real, age-integrated world to such an extent that he may actually be raised by his age-mates. According to their observations, the American child usually grows up in an atmosphere pervaded by a subtle opposition of his peers to the standards of adult society, an opposition that is persuasive. The result is called "peer dependency," and it has already reached major proportions.

Identity, Security, and the Rock

The issue in social development, and in peer dependency, is one of identity. Personal identity is a major factor in all human experience. A child yearns for the security that comes from knowing who he is. But how do we ever know who we are? It is by knowing how we relate to the persons, places, and things around us. We find our identity in our relationships.

I am secure in my identity because, while most of my relationships are relatively stable, the first of them is absolutely unbreakable. My life, including my identity, is built upon the "rock" of my relationship to Jesus Christ (Matthew 7:24). If some of the other relationships should come to an end, the rock will always remain.

Our Father in heaven designed into us this need to have a secure identity based upon a set of stable relationships. No temporal ties can take the place of our eternal salvation in Christ. But in Christ there are many other relationships worth having. Family, church, hometown, vocation, and national relationships give a continuity to life that adds to our sense of security. They support our continued mental, emotional, and spiritual health.

Take these relationships away from us, and, unless we really "know whom we have believed," we will behave like anyone else who loses his identity. We will go searching for new relationships to serve as security substitutes for the relationships we have lost.

So peer dependency is nothing less than an identity problem. Having been uprooted too early from his family, church, and neighborhood relationships, the youngster is forced to go foraging through his school activities for substitute relationships with which to construct his identity. School groups, gangs, and cliques are often the child's security substitutes. To the degree that the child becomes emotionally entangled in the new substitutes, he is likely to become "peer-dependent."

Signs of Peer Dependency

Studies in the sociological effects of age-segregated, peer-group interaction confirm what common sense and observation reveal. Children who spend greater amounts of time with a peer group than with their own parents tend to become emotionally dependent on their peer group. When this happens, the following behavior is commonly reported:

1. The child tends to hold to the norms and values of his peer group, over and above those of the parental team. When faced with a conflict between the standards of his parents and those of his peers at school, the child seeks ways to meet the group's demands without provoking discipline from his

parents. His tastes in dress, hair, music, food, toys, and vocabulary fall into line with his group's standards. Less noticeable are changes in the child's attitude toward family standards in faith and morality.

Once the child's tastes are being heavily affected by his group, the child tends to become a victim of more deep-seated social contagion. Various behaviors and vocabulary are freely passed around the group. Leaders in the peer group, often the most rebellious to begin with, start testing their powers over each member by asking outlandish things of them. The choice is always the same: conform or be rejected.

2. If the peer-dependent child continues along this course, spending greater amounts of time with his age-mates, he is likely to become incapable of holding to his family's values in the face of peer-group opposition. This is called an "ethical cave-in." Psychosocial forces quickly bind the child to a degree of conformity that is destructive to his personality. He cannot confess Christ before men.

3. Such a child's sense of personal worth and hope for his own future may be distorted by his haphazard experiences of cruel rejection, on the one hand, and unwarranted popularity on the other. A "house of mirrors," comprised of each group-member's distorted perception of the child, convinces him that he is what they perceive him to be. He lacks the self-confidence to even doubt it.

Bound with a warped image of his own personality, he begins to faithfully process all further experiences in ways that support his group-constructed self-perception. His life may become a self-fulfilling prophecy, proving again and again that the group was right. The tightly wound threads of his childhood experience may continue to bind him for the rest of his life.

Are children and teenagers genetically destined to seek out and join social groupings of their age-mates as a means of securing an identity? History tells us "No! It hasn't always been this way."

Before the age-segregated classroom school became popular in the 1880's, we have little sign of age peer-groupings. Why did the schools separate into age-graded classes? The answer is, to save money.

In order to use women as elementary school teachers (at half the cost of a male teacher), public and private school administrators had to remove the older, more uncontrollable students from the classes with younger students — enter age segregation. The idea was attacked by many educators as "lockstep." It forced students into an artificial pace with the proverbial "average student."

In practice, age grading seldom lined up with the student's actual study level in any subject. Age has little to do with one's aptitude for math or reading. But the financial advantages were overpowering. Within a few years, schools across the nation accepted the age-graded approach. Elementary teaching became a woman's profession, and childhood has since been an age-segregated experience.

Social Development in the Home School

The choice between peer dependency and positive social development involves more than a decision to keep the child out of conventional schooling. Childhood, like creation, hates a vacuum. If we succeed only in taking away the influence of the peer group, we do only half the job of Godly parenting.

The other half is to fill our child's life with a firm foundation on the Rock of his personal salvation, family relationships, and social experiences that strengthen his sense of identity and sharpen his ability to exert a Godly influence in the world. Home schooling requires of parents the positive initiative to give their children the very best in all areas of Christian education.

Early Socialization
by James C. Dobson, Ph.D., *Focus on the Family*

I have been increasingly concerned during the past 10 years about the damage done to our children by one another.

When I revised my book, *Hide or Seek,* I added 30 pages and devoted them to the theme, "Teaching children to be kind." I stated my convictions therein that the epidemic of inferiority and inadequacy seen during the teen years is rooted in the ridicule, rejection, and social competition experienced by vulnerable young children. They are simply not ready to handle the threats to the self-concept that are common in any elementary setting.

I have seen kids dismantle one another, while parents and teachers passively stood by and observed the "socialization" process. I've then watched the recipients of this pressure begin to develop defense mechanisms and coping strategies that should never be necessary in a young child.

Dr. Urie Bronfenbrenner verified the validity of this concern in his study of sixth-grade children and younger. He found that those who spent less of their elective time with their parents than their peers tended to become peer dependent.

Dozens of other investigations have demonstrated, at least to my satisfaction, the error of the notion that children must be exposed to other children in order to be properly socialized. I just don't believe it.

In fact, the opposite is true. They need the security and love of parental protection and guidance until their self-concepts are more stabilized and established.

Perhaps we've all been led into believing something that isn't best for kids. In fact, maybe our own tendency to jerk little children from the security of their homes at an earlier and earlier age is related to the agitation and self-doubt that is so common in the drug-infested, alcohol-abusing generation of teenagers today.

Obviously we're doing something wrong, when the vast majority of adolescents emerge from high school with intense personal dissatisfaction and feelings of inferiority.

In summary, I believe the home school is the wave of the future. In addition to many advantages, it provides a third alternative to a humanistic public school and an expensive or nonexistent Christian school in a given area.

Should Christians Ever Disobey Civil Law?

This may become one of the most important issues of the Christian's testimony in this decade! Currently, there is wide disagreement concerning civil disobedience in the church and among home schooling families.

For instance, we have one group of home schoolers who believe Christians should always obey their government and then trust in God for their deliverance. On the surface, this appears to be a very spiritual position.

On the other end of the spectrum are those Christians who are nearly anti-government. They have determined that parents are responsible to God alone for their children's upbringing and that government has no rights in this area. These parents tend to be almost paranoid, believing that every government or school official is possibly demonic. They then dare all officials by openly challenging the officials' presumed authority. These poor parents remind me of Peter cutting off the ear of the priest's slave when they came to arrest Jesus (i.e. ready to fight at the wrong time).

Doesn't Each Group Have Scriptural Support?

Isn't it true that Christians are to submit to the govenment God sets over them? YES! (Matthew 22:21; Romans 13:1-7)

But isn't it also true that parents are the only God-appointed authorities over their own children? YES! (Psalms 127:3; Deuteronomy 6:7; Proverbs 22:6; Ephesians 6:4)

PROBLEM: When government over-steps the parents' authority, what does the submissive Christian do?

Obviously we are not to submit like a bunch of dumb sheep to a government that seeks to take our life or the lives of our children. (The Hebrew babies were saved by disobedience through a lie in Exodus 1:16-22; Moses was saved by disobedience in Exodus 2:1-3; the Christ child was saved by escape from the country in Matthew 2:12-14; and Paul was delivered in Acts 9:23-25)

APPLICATION: If a particular state's laws prevent the family from fulfilling the Biblical commands to teach or train their children according to the Word of God, then leaving that state is one option.

Just as obvious Scripturally, we are not authorized to revolt against or attempt to overthrow our state or national government. Revolution is *never* authorized by the Word of God as an option. However, overt disobedience *is* commanded as a testimony when government interferes with our worship of God (Acts 5:29) such as:

1. Demands false worship (Dan. 3:10-12; 16-18; Rev. 14:9-13).
2. Prevents worship of God (Dan. 6:7-11; 6:21).
3. Prevents teaching of the Word (Acts 4:18-20; 5:29; Jer. 37 & 38).
4. Demands that you violate a direct command of God—commit murder, steal, bring false testimony, not use corporal punishment on your children, etc. (Acts 5:29).

These are the points where a believer is expected to make a *non-violent* stand, even to the point of martyrdom.

Make sure that if you go to jail, or have to go to court, that your testimony brings glory to God. The observing unbeliever should be able to see that *your obedience to God* was clearly the issue of your stand. (Look at the testimony of the believer in *Chariots of Fire*. Even though unbelievers may not have agreed with the hero's stand, they did honor his testimony before God.)

Your personal opinions, personal standards, or your political position is not to be the issue. The fact that government is "wrong" in its position is *not* sufficient reason for a *religious* stand! Our stand must not be made on the basis of what we *fear* government *might* do, but on the reality of something we *are* required to do that is truly against the Word of God. (I Tim. 6:1; Tit.3:1,2)

"For God hath not given us the spirit of fear; but of power, and of love, and of a sound mind." (II Tim. 1:7; cf Hb. 13:6) (Many Christians make an emotional stand too early on political issues and just look like religious nuts!)

Summary

A Christian should submit to his govenment unless it actually interferes with his worship or obedience to God, or threatens his family's life; then the Christian can either leave that government's jurisdiction, or stay and take a firm stand on God's Word for a testimony to unbelievers.

NOTE: Nowhere in Scripture do I see believers encouraged by God to set up an underground movement. Cowardliness is not a Christlike testimony.

How About Our Political Rights?

Don't be confused and think that Christians are guaranteed good government. The book of Judges reveals that God allows man to have exactly the kind of government he deserves: cruel and oppressive when believers are uncommitted; just and benevolent when they make God the center of their life. God never guaranteed that the pillar of freedom America once was would last forever! But, as long as we have the opportunity, Christians should exercise their Constitutional responsibilities as citizens. It is not unsubmissive for a Christian in America to go to court against a state government for its violation of his constitutional rights. In fact, it is his duty.

Under our constitutional form of government, *all* parents, Christian and non-Christian, have rights which can be defended — all the way to the Supreme Court. This is true at the Federal level all the way down to the least significant official in a state government. Your rights can even be defended against the myriad of unofficial bureaucrats who assume limitless authority until stopped.

The right of parents to control the education of their own children is protected by the U.S. Constitution under:

- Freedom of speech
- The freedom of religion
- The right to privacy

The Constitution doesn't even mention the issue of education for children, leaving this matter entirely in the hands of the parents.

Common law has held that parents had total authority over their children's education from at least the 1700's as was first written in *Blackstone's Commentaries*. This position has been stedfastly upheld by the courts in America for the past two hundred years. The Supreme Court has consistently overruled state laws in 1925 (Pierce vs. Society of Sisters), 1927, and 1972 (Yoder) in favor of parental liberty over their children's education.

Several state supreme courts and also many lower courts have upheld parental rights against alleged state's interests up to this very day. (See *Home Education and Constitutional Law*, by Whitehead.) Even though most states have adopted their own laws concerning public education, many of these laws are unconstitutional in regards to the home school. If, in a state's law, home education isn't considered equal to "private education," has non-absolute "equivalency" requirements, requires a certified teacher, and many other issues, that state's law is unconstitutional.

Remember, no legitimate authority has been granted by U.S. law for state's rights in the matter of education to be above the rights of the parent. (States have granted these rights to themselves and some state laws are still uncontested.) States must also prove any "compelling interests" to have it their way, and prove that their solution is the least burdensome. No state possesses the compelling interest for the education of your child! God didn't give it to them, the U.S. Constitution didn't, the federal government hasn't yet. Parents alone have a compelling interest in educating their own children to satisfy God's requirements. It is not only their right, it is their responsibility.

However, it should be pointed out that many liberal judges do not accept the U. S. Constitution, as originally written, to be the law of the land. These judges may rule contrary to our constitutional rights at any time. We must be willing to test these rulings or lose the guarantee of our freedom.

What Is The Source of Our Rights?

God-given/
Inalienable Right: Non-transferrable, inherent, uncontestable human right given by God to all men (your individual freedom: life, liberty, and the pursuit of happiness).

Constitutional Right: A civil right as decided by men that cannot easily be changed (absolute law). However, it can be misinterpreted or ignored by judges.

Statutory Right: Civil law, a right granted by a civil government for the moment (can be changed by whim).

Obviously, the closer to a God-given, inalienable right a law is, the more permanent it is; while civil laws are very unstable and can be changed at will by politicians.

What Should You Do About Your State's Laws on Home Schooling?

1. Cooperate openly at each stage of statutory law while resting in the fact that you are merely volunteering submission, but not under the authority of the arbitrary law. (Submitting to state requirements which allow you to teach your children at home — like registration, or achievement testing which do not violate your proper worship of God — establishes your good-faith effort to cooperate.) Actively work within the political system to make the laws "right." This includes even "going to court" if necessary.

2. Be prepared to leave the state or to challenge the law when it declares, for instance, that you *cannot* teach your own children or that you *must* teach anti-God texts. But, only if you are being prevented from fulfilling your *Biblically provable responsibilities.* When you do challenge a non-Biblical law, be prepared to go all the way and be a positive testimony to God before the unbelievers. Remember, every Christian martyr in history, as well as each signer of the U.S. Constitution, suffered severe monetary loss or loss of life. They were willing to die for what they believed in. I believe that Christians will be called on to stand up and be counted for their beliefs more and more in the coming years.

If we make a stand prematurely, we bring unnecessary, self-induced pressure on ourselves. We also appear as rebels and thus do not glorify God. However, if we fail to stand (no matter what the personal cost *might* be) when our obedience to God is clearly challenged, we lose the opportunity for a testimony to God and our Lord.

Example

Let's say your state is like Arizona and requires the following:

1. The home school teacher must take and pass a proficiency exam in reading, grammar, and math. (A simple, 8th grade level test that any competent high school graduate should pass.)

2. Parents must file an affidavit with the county school superintendent annually, stating that their child is being taught at home. The results of a standardized achievement test must be submitted each year.

3. Parents must also file proof of the child's birth.

Now what do you do? Let's analyze the believer's position on this issue. 1. Does the state have a Constitutional right for any of these statutes? Absolutely not! Education is not mentioned in the Constitution and the U. S. Supreme Court has not yet changed the Constitution by their ruling. 2. Does the state have a right to enforce compulsory attendance? Not by the Constitution or historical common law. But by the fact that they have passed this law, they have given themselves that right. 3. Is the state asking a believer to violate any passage of Scripture, like "thou shalt not reveal thy children's names and ages to the Philistines," or "never reveal thy ignorance nor that of thy children before the uncircumcised." Obviously, someone would have to stretch a long way to make the state's statutes a spiritual issue. The rebellious of heart probably just desire to avoid accountibility to anyone. This is especially true for those who have adopted an unstructured methodology.

Christians seem to live in mortal fear that government is more satanic than anything else. Government is God's institution designed for *us!* So, obey the statutes and be the best testimony you can of a Christian family submitting to God's government. But what if the parent fails the test? Study and take it again! If you have older children (7th-12th grades) reevaluate your ability to teach them with your apparent deficiencies. If you are just a lousy test taker and sure you could teach your grade school children 1. ask for an exemption based on the young age of your children, 2. move, 3. satellite school under a Christian school, 4. hire a tutor. In other words, as long as there is an acceptable means to meet our God-given responsibilities, the Biblical command to submit to government still applies.

What if the state tells me my children's achievement tests don't indicate sufficient teaching has occurred and it won't accept my affidavit for next year? You still have options: 1. tutor, 2. Christian school, 3. satellite group, 4. move. Then submit your affidavit for the next year. It seems there are almost always options for those who try to find them. Obviously, the rebels never look for solutions. They just live in fear of getting caught for needless rebellion.

If these examples are not satisfactory to explain where the spiritual line can be drawn against government's power, please write me. I sincerely want to communicate these important principles. There may come a day when our governments really do try to take away our Christian rights. When that time comes, I'll be right there to draw the line. But for now, Satan's war is with man's words and principles; and our doubts and fears. Obedience to the Word is our surest deliverance.

Steps To Avoid Legal Problems

1. Find out what your state and local laws are, as well as what the attitude of your local superintendent of schools is toward home schooling. This is most easily accomplished by contacting your state's home school association. I recommend that you join and support these associations for the information and benefits available from coordinated group action. If you can't locate a group, write to the *Home School Legal Defense Association* for the name and address of the associations in your state. They can also provide you with the most current information on the legal status of home schooling in your state.

2. Establish credibility for your home school in one of several ways:

   a. Enroll your children in a correspondence school that will provide testing and placement services, record keeping, and consulting. Cost is from $120 to $180 per student per year, plus curriculum costs, testing, and registration fees. This should be done if you are unsure about your ability to educate your children and have no formal support group or active home school association with members near enough to offer you moral support and occasional advice.

   b. Enroll your family in a formal support group, ideally one composed of other members of your own local church and led by a coordinator with the proven talent or spiritual gift of administration. This coordinator would assist each family with testing and placement and may order curriculum for everyone, arrange for specialists for academic help, and provide a regular program to help ensure student progress. Cost is from $10 to $25 per month per family, unless the coordinator is also providing tutoring services in addition to the administrative service. Then the monthly fee should be about $10 to $25 per month per child. Any ministering Christian school should be willing to work with you as a satellite of its ministry.

c. Join the *Home School Legal Defense Association* and carefully follow its recommendations for keeping attendance and student progress records. Warning! Join *before* you are contacted by any official group. Cost is $100 per family per year and is essential for anyone not enrolled in one of the previous two plans detailed in *a.* and *b.* It is also recommended for anyone living in a state where laws are unfavorable to home schooling, even if they are enrolled in plan *a.* or *b.* Approximately 90% of all contacts with school districts, truant officers, and prosecutors are resolved by HSLDA attorneys without going to court. If your family must go to court, HSLDA will hire a local attorney familiar with constitutional defenses and education laws, and will pay all attorney fees. Write to HSLDA, Paeonian Springs, VA 22129, for an application.

3. Study the home school position so that you become an expert on the issues of socialization, parents' God-given rights and abilities to educate their children, and other issues in order to gain confidence to deal with those who are less informed. This knowledge will also increase your own commitment to home schooling.

a. Start by subscribing to the magazine, *The Teaching Home*, P.O. Box 20219, Portland, OR 97220-0219. This bimonthly newsletter contains invaluable articles on everything about home schooling. You will especially want all of their reprinted articles and all of the back issues you can obtain.

b. Prepare yourself spiritually to stand firm if under attack. Read, J. Richard Fugate's, *What the Bible Says About...Child Training*, John W. Whitehead and Wendell R. Bud's, *Home Education and Constitutional Liberties*, and Mike Farris' (HSLDA president), *Should Home Schoolers Obey the Law?*

c. Attend local, state, and national home school conventions for fellowship, new curriculum awareness, and inspiration.

Reasons for Support Groups

I would recommend that every home school family join or start a support group as soon as possible after beginning their home schooling adventure.

Ideally, your church leadership would sponsor, or at least would be supportive of, a home school satellite program or support group.

Organizing the home school families at your church will make it easy to locate other home school families who share not only your same needs but who agree with you in doctrine. A formal support group will benefit you by:

- enabling you to learn from others who have gone before. "A wise man will hear, and will increase learning; and a man of understanding shall attain unto wise counsels" (Proverbs 1:5).

- encouraging you to remain steadfast in your commitment. "Now we exhort you brethren, ...support the weak ...." (I Thessalonians 5:14).

- pooling the gifts and talents of many parents. "As every man hath received the gift, even so minister the same one to another, as good stewards of the manifold grace of God" (I Peter 4:10).

- providing fellowship for both adults and children. "And let us consider one another to provoke unto love and to good words: Not forsaking the assembling of ourselves together, as the manner of some is; but exhorting one another: and so much the more, as ye see the day approaching" (Hebrews 10:24,25).

- being a vehicle where local vision can emerge. "Where there is no vision the people perish ..." (Proverbs 29:18).

I firmly believe that local, organized groups—whether based around a church, a Christian school, or a well-run community group—are essential to the on-going strength of the home school movement.

Extension programs set up by local Christian schools for home schoolers are especially helpful for high-school-age children who benefit from academic assistance with higher level courses.

Satan is certainly against any plan that will strengthen the family. He will attack it directly through government, the NEA, etc., and internally through our doubt, insecurity, and lack of commitment.

Isolation can also work against standing up for God's plan.

Remember that Elijah, after he had served God greatly, requested that he might die! He said, "I, I only, am left, and they seek my life, to take it away."(I Kings 19:10)

In isolation, Elijah became extremely depressed just after he had been used mightily by God. God informed him that He had 7,000 other souls in Israel. Elijah had never been really alone, but he had no contact with others and therefore thought it was all up to him. A good support group ends this feeling of isolation and replaces it with one of unified effort.

The Most Important
Benefits of Home Schooling

Families new to home schooling often ask, "What benefits does a child derive from being taught at home?" Those who have successfully home schooled for several years can readily answer: closer family relationships, protection from ungodly peer influence and false teaching, superior education, and correctly balanced socialization.

While these four important benefits are definitely true, I believe there is an even more important benefit - both the child and his parents can become more mature!

It is my firm conviction that being successful in home schooling demands proper child training. I also believe that the most successful parents are those who allow God to train *them* as well. Thus, parent and child should benefit greatly from the experience of home schooling.

The likelihood of producing a well-trained child is enhanced when both of his parents are committed to educating him. This is true partly because requiring a child to do school work and to learn will often conflict with his immaturity. A child's nature may exhibit willfullness, pride, or laziness under the pressure of regular school work, even though his parents are reasonable in their requirements, particularly when a child is coming out of the limited requirements of a classroom.

The successful parent is one who will consistently deal with these soul problems when they occur. This training is more important than academic teaching. Parents should be careful not to be influenced by humanistic methods that actually avoid these problem areas. Behavior modification's solution to a child's resistance is to back off the pressure and either use techniques to manipulate the child or reduce the assignment. However, avoiding conflict with your child will never train him. When a child's sinful nature manifests itself, it must be challenged and overcome if you are going to be successful in training your child "in the way he should go."

Parents become more mature by just surviving a few years of home schooling. Their pride is humbled by seeing how much they don't know. Their willfullness is controlled by self sacrifice. Their laziness is replaced with self discipline and industry when required to hold down the equivalent of a second job.

Effective home schooling means that a mother must give up most of her discretionary time and also become more organized than a business manager. It also means that a husband must give up some of his wife's attention to him and function more as a father and family team member than ever before. These temporary sacrifices are inconsequential compared to their own personal growth and their children's development which will benefit them throughout their lives.

I believe all home schooling parents who apply themselves to the task "as unto the Lord," will become increasingly more mature in the process. Conversely, parents who don't allow their natural weaknesses to be challenged and trained are very likely to quit home schooling because of the continuous irritation it will be to their natures. Either that or they will do a superficial job of teaching and training to the detriment of their children.

A normal child should progress at least one year for each year of study as measured by an objective test, such as any of the standardized tests. Progress of one year to one and a half years per year of study would not be unreasonable for an average to above average child, even through all twelve grade levels. Remember, college entrance at thirteen years of age was the norm in our country in the 1800's.

Parents need to establish long-range objectives for each child commensurate with his own abilities, assign the work load necessary to reach those objectives, and then monitor each child's progress often to determine that the objectives are reasonable and adjust them accordingly.

I truly believe that home schooling should protect the child from Satanic false teaching and peer pressure. In addition to this, home schooling is perhaps the best way for parents to train their children to become mature, responsible adults willing to live their lives for God. However, I believe God intends for home schooling to affect the lives of parents every bit as much as that of their children. The husband and wife team who work together to produce morally trained, well educated, and spiritually alert children will produce a work of extreme eternal value. These parents will also be personally blessed as the rigorous task of achieving these results produces a maturity in themselves that will enable them to be what the Bible refers to as "he who overcomes the world" – in others words, true winners in life.

SECTION II

GENERAL INFORMATION

The articles in this section deal with the reasons some parents fail in their home schooling experience. Also covered are two important philosophical issues: should Christians use educational tests and should pressure ever be applied to a student? I believe this information may prevent many parents from failing in their home schooling attempt if they understand the pitfalls from the beginning.

Why Educational Testing?

Should Christian parents be concerned with standardized testing of their children? They certainly should understand the issues before making their decisions. An overview of the subject of student testing from the theological, philosophical, and practical perspective will assist parents in reaching this understanding.

Theological Perspective

God's Word makes it clear that all believers (as His children) are meant to be tested for the purpose of their refinement, resulting in His approval (I Chronicles 29:17; Job 23:10; Psalm 11:5; I Thessalonians 2:4).

God tests His childrens':

1) Thinking and emotions (Psalm 7:9; 139:23; Proverbs 17:3; I Thessalonians 2:4).

2) Work (production) (I Corinthians 3:13), and

3) Faith (knowledge and use of the Word) to conquer temptation (I Peter 1:7; 4:12; James 1:3).

Human parents are responsible for training their children according to God's Word and have been delegated the authority to do so (Deut. 6:1-9; Psalm 127:3; Proverbs 22:6; Matthew 15:4; Romans 13:1; Ephesians 6:4; Colossians 3:20).

Therefore, it seems apparent from the theological viewpoint that parents should also examine and evaluate students' academically and spiritually throughout their growth (Proverbs 20:11).

Philosophical Perspective

Some Christians object to any kind of standardized testing for several reasons:

- because the child's score is compared with the average of other students of the same grade level who have taken the test. Some Christians believe this process promotes the false thought that man is just a form of social animal and that fitting in with the group as average is the optimum goal.

- because they fear that government's interpretation of these test results may lead to their children being forced to return to public school, or even worse, being taken away.

- because they believe that children should not be compared with one another (II Corinthians 10:12).

While these all may be *bona fide* concerns, they do not properly consider the legitimate reasons for testing. Proper testing should assist in evaluating where a student *is* in his academic progress for optimum placement and reveal how much progress has occurred.

There are basically two types of standardized academic tests: learning ability and achievement. Standarized tests compare one student's results to a group of other children of the same age.

- **Learning ability tests are designed to be predictive.** In other words, they are meant to measure a child's capability at that time and to predict at what point in academic materials he or she ought to be able to progress successfully. Learning ability tests are sometimes called intelligence, aptitude, or mental ability tests. Examples of this type of test are the ICAT (Iowa Cognitive Abilities Test) and the Otis-Lennon School Ability Test. A learning ability test attempts to measure a child's natural talents so we can know how far to challenge him, but also where to let up (Colossians 3:23; Philippians 3:12; Matthew 25:15-28; I Corinthians 10:13).

- **Achievement tests are designed to be descriptive.** In other words, they are meant to indicate what a child has learned previously when compared to a broad base of other students. Examples of achievement tests are CAT, SAT, Iowa TBS, and MAT.

Please take note that standardized tests are not precise instruments of measurement, but rather tools to be used wisely. The data collected can be evaluated for the student's academic strengths and weaknesses and for general information. However, consideration must be given to the fact that this data only reveals how well a student performed on a particular day, and as compared to a composite of 500,000 or so other students from varying ethnic, cultural, and family backgrounds. The usefulness of the data also depends on how well the test administrator followed the instructions, and on the interpreter's knowledge of the specific test given.

Also to be considered is the year of the test. Each test is rewritten about every six to eight years and is based on the textbooks in use at the time the version is compiled. In other words, a 1989 released test (like the SAT 8) will be written on the currently most often used books in major cities nationwide. Therefore, achievement tests attempt to measure how well these textbooks and/or teachers have taught material covered in these books. Obviously, an achievement test should relate to the textbooks a student has been studying to be valid. There is a real question whether secular standardized tests have any validity at all evaluating Christian children who don't use modern textbooks. Even though standardized tests have definite short comings, determining what a student has learned can be helpful in teaching effectively. Parents should learn how best to use these tools in order to be the most effective teachers possible.

Practical Perspective

Parents have several important reasons to test children who are new to home schooling. The most important of these reasons is to know where a child is in his educational experience. The most valuable test for determining this point is a diagnostic test. This test should be administered before a child begins to home school. The diagnostic test is ideal to use because it will tell you exactly what your child's academic strengths and weaknesses are. You can then choose curricula at a level to match the academic profile of your child. A diagnostic test does not compare one child's knowledge with the knowledge of other children. Instead it relates his knowledge directly to a particular scope and sequence of learning objectives. For example, if the diagnostic test reveals a weakness in fourth grade addition of fractions, you can tailor the curriculum choice to meet this need. This matching process greatly enhances your success and ability to motivate the child.

Another reason to test is to measure advancement on a regular basis. Any standard achievement test can be used in this way. When administered one full year after the first testing date and every year thereafter, it should indicate what the student has learned each year. Remember, the first year's testing is only a reference point for future years and should not be depended on for original placement. If the later tests are not positive (like only six months progress each year), changes should be considered with the method or curriculum as necessary.

The third reason to use standardized tests is to be prepared for state and county government, school officials, and even court, if necessary. No conscientious educator should fear showing the results of his work. Your students will probably exceed the national average in every subject! National statistics show that Christian school and home school students' usually average about one and one-half years above their public school counterparts.

College Entrance

Most community, A&M, and independent colleges will accept students graduating from home schools with a SAT score of 1000 or more. Any student of average intellect who has been home schooled properly for three or four years should easily pass. In my opinion any competent 9th grader who has completed that grade could easily score above 1000 points. However, most state colleges and universities will blackball home schoolers since they don't come from accredited schools.

Conclusion

Standardized tests and especially diagnostic tests have their place in the educational development of a child. However, these tests should **never** be viewed as anything more than a tool. The best test should measure knowledge according to a set standard or criterion, not other students' knowledge. Proper use of these tests enables a parent to better understand their child's needs and how to help him or her progress. Therefore, tests can be a vital part of "training up a child in the way he should go."

Should Pressure Ever Be Used in Teaching?

If this is your first year of home schooling, you may be having some second thoughts by now. That precious child you used to send off to school and almost never had any trouble with has changed. She is now more stubborn and temperamental than you ever thought possible. What has happened? Are you doing something wrong? Maybe home schooling isn't right for your child?

Let me put your mind at ease. This is not an unusual problem for new home schoolers at all. In fact, the only way to avoid it entirely would be never to require a child to perform beyond his or her own desires. In other words, if your son doesn't want to slow down and pronounce his words correctly, just let him slur them over for now, hoping that someday he will magically develop enough self-discipline to do it on his own. Or, if your daughter is stubborn about learning her multiplication tables, just let it slide for now. Maybe someday when she is "ready," those tables will be easy and fun for her to learn. After all, some educational experts promote such a philosophy of non-pressured learning. Obviously, teaching would be a much easier task with this approach. If a child is never required to do what he doesn't wish to do, many conflicts can definitely be avoided.

So then, what is wrong with this *laissez-faire* approach to education? First, this approach only works with children who are internally motivated (and then in only those areas in which they have personal interest) or with those children who can be manipulated through their strong desire or need for parental approval. Second, this approach avoids the much needed challenge to a child's soul weaknesses — pride, laziness, or rebellion.

Education, after all, requires effort. It can not be all fun. Being required to memorize formulas, paradigms, and the *Gettysburg Address* builds character and teaches self-discipline and self-confidence, which are learned behaviors not inherited ones. When parents do not demand any more from their children than the children wish to give, they short-circuit that character development. Remember, some of the most valuable lessons most of us learned were the ones we learned under pressure.

When my wife and I removed our children from public and private schools, we carefully tested each of them to know for ourselves what they needed. We were shocked to find that our graduating 7th grader, who was in the advanced class at public school, couldn't even handle 5th grade mathematics or grammar skills and was virtually illiterate. For the first several months of home schooling, one half of each day was spent on phonics, reading history, and science lessons at the 6th grade level with a dictionary at her side. In the public school she was told just to skip over the words she couldn't read! At home we found she couldn't pronounce most multisyllable words and did not know the meaning of over 50% of "everyday" words. Every night she was also required to read aloud to us for about one hour from her day's work. She had to pronounce each word correctly and know the meaning of every word. Of course this meant that during the day she had to look up almost every word in the dictionary, sound it out phonetically, and learn its meaning. There was literally much weeping and gnashing of teeth for the first several months, but we loved our daughter enough to keep on paying the cost. She tried complaining, whining, and everything short of overt rebellion to cause us to back down and let her remain ignorant. Eventually she became a competent reader, excellent in math skills, and an extremely self-confident person. Yes, she did graduate from high school a couple of years "behind" at 19 years of age, but she then scored as a Junior in college on her S.A.T. in all subjects.

Let me digress for a moment and discuss an issue brought up by our taking our daughter back in her studies and by delaying her graduation until age 19. I wish parents could rid themselves of the totally meaningless term, "grade level."

Some parents seem obsessed with what "grade" their child is supposed to be in, or over what day public school starts, or by trying to match other administrative rules developed for the school's own convenience. The purpose of education is to have students learn. The number of days children attend classes, or what time school starts, or what grade they should be in by a particular age has little to do with the amount of learning that takes place. You don't need to violate any state laws, but please don't let simply arbitrary rules restrict you from properly educating your children.

The example of my daughter's need to overcome the terrible lack of education she had received and the poor attitude toward any real study she had developed is a severe case. It is, however, a common one when teens are taken out of public school. Therefore, please understand that not all learning must be accomplished under pressure. Some learning can be enjoyable, but enjoyment itself should not be the objective! Parents need not be overly concerned that they are making every lesson "exciting," "fun," or even interesting. Real life isn't that way and it is highly misleading to prepare a child for adulthood with that distorted viewpoint.

No matter how much a parent tries to avoid conflict in learning, it will eventually show up. Most children will naturally experience both easy and difficult learning periods. Individual children will respond to different subjects in a variety of ways. One child will enjoy dashing through his math until he hits a section he doesn't comprehend and then will balk like a donkey on this difficult section. Another child may get bored easily with non-challenging work but obviously enjoy a challenging timed-race on that same subject. It will be at these points of reluctance, or even out-right rebellion against the work of learning, that a parent is confronted with an important decision. "Should I apply pressure in this learning situation, or not?"

If you are experiencing a great deal of conflict with your children, consider the possibility that they may be working in curriculum that is beyond their present abilities. There are plenty of tests available to help you determine what your child knows and the skill level he should be able to handle. If he is placed in materials too difficult for him, just to be "on grade level," by all means place him properly and above all don't worry about the grade level. It is cruel to make a child try to perform in material beyond his ability and it causes frustration, impatience, feelings of being dumb, worthless, and a failure. However, if the conflict you are experiencing is simply because you expect him to achieve in accordance with his known abilities, may God support you in applying all the pressure needed to train your child. Once the reluctant child learns that you will accept nothing less than due diligence on his school work (as well as on his chores around the house) he will have developed the first stage of self-control. Your life as a parent will be much easier, and even joyful, as your children become more responsible and mature under your training. And, home schooling will have been the instrument of that training.

For a complete discussion on the philosophy behind, and fallicies with, delayed education read, *Will Early Education Ruin Your Child?* This booklet examines the "proofs" for delaying and never pushing a child to learn. It also compares the humanistic philosophy behind that theory with Biblical truths.

Will Early Education Ruin Your Child?
by J. Richard Fugate
Available from Alpha Omega Publishers and Christian bookstores. ISBN#0-86717-006-9

Potential Stumbling Blocks to Home Schooling

Along with many other potential problems encountered in home schooling, there is the matter of fathers who have not been involved in their children's home education. This is a very serious problem and one that threatens the very existence of the home school movement.

When a father does not understand the evils of humanism and the dangers of immoral peer pressure on his children or the Biblical reasons to avoid secular education at any cost, he is not likely to support home schooling, let alone to become involved. In these families it is usually the mother who has become interested in home schooling. She may have been motivated solely by the philosophy currently popular in some Christian circles of keeping children out of formal schooling until they are 8 to 10 years old. If so, the father who does not understand the other, larger issues involved will probably only tolerate home schooling for those few years.

A more difficult problem is when a mother continues to become more knowledgeable on the broader issues affecting home schooling, while the father does not. Few men read consistently, so it is quite easy for wives to get ahead of their husbands in this area. Unfortunately, most wives don't know how to handle this position without intimidating their husbands.

However, husbands usually can be patiently brought along to the wives' level of knowledge by reading together or discussing books like *The Battle for the Mind* by Tim LaHaye, and the wife asking for the husband's opinions and advice. She could take him to a Christian Life Workshop, conducted by Gregg Harris, or to any good teaching on family renewal, and then patiently wait.

It may take time, but the result will not only be involvement— it will be leadership. When a mother moves ahead without the father's active participation, she should not be surprised when he remains uninvolved. If he was not involved in the fact-finding and original decision, it is likely that he won't be involved in the follow-through.

Other Stumbling Blocks

Three of the biggest concerns parents have after they have been home schooling for a while are: how to organize and manage each day, how to control their children's willful natures, and how to control themselves so that they can exercise the self-discipline to handle the first two concerns.

Many of us were raised by the permissive philosophy of child rearing, i.e., don't restrict a child's desires and don't ever challenge his will. Indeed, there are even some Christian educators who carry this undisciplined, *"lazy"fare* approach into the field of academics.

You may have personally experienced a lack of training in your childhood that resulted in poor self discipline and a willful, self-centered attitude that you have been battling all of your adult life. Therefore, one obstacle to overcome in home schooling is ourselves. If we are undisciplined, we will not be very successful in teaching our children.

However, any parent can be more successful in home schooling by setting up a few simple external controls over themselves and their children. Joining a good support group could help. Preferably it will be one that promotes accountability for student progress (like a minimum of one year's improvement in each subject per year).

Most importantly, you should work on the root of the problem—your own character. We can all become more successful teachers by first coming to understand ourselves. Study some of the Christian self-help books like: *Telling Yourself the Truth* by William Backus and Marie Chapian, for those of you who have convinced yourself that you can't change or that you can't do anything right; or *Sidetracked Home Executive* by Pam Young and Peggy Jones, for those who think they can't ever get organized. Finally study, *What the Bible Says About...Child Training*, to learn about the child training **you** may still need as well as that which your children definitely still need.

The stumbling blocks listed and any others can serve to challenge us toward self-improvement and a better life. It all depends on what we do about them – trip over them, or overcome them.

Needed: a Few Good Men

(For Dads Only)

It is my opinion that our country is sadly lacking male leadership today in every area of life. Beginning with the family and moving to the church, business, and finally, government, we are experiencing an ever increasing need for true leaders — men who have vision, who are willing to give the sacrifice of service, and who have the character necessary to give direction.

What has happened? Men used to be proud of their role of leadership. Why have the men of the last two generations abdicated their roles? I have often pondered this question and would like to suggest the following possibility.

I believe that most of a nation's problems can be traced to the family — to values taught and the examples lived. There was a dramatic change in the American family shortly after World War II. Prosperity and materialism became the order of the day. There was plenty of work and more things available to purchase than ever before in mankind's history. Many adults had grown up in deprivation, having lived through a severe depression as children. They had sacrificed through the war with rationing and having only the absolute necessities. Now they could have it *all* after 20 years of want!

But to get it, the men would have to work extra hours, go back to school to improve their education, or take a second job. A few wives kept the jobs they had obtained due to the severe shortage of men, especially in factories essential to the war effort. Most women, however, returned home. Men and women still believed that it was the man's responsibility to provide for his family's needs and protection and that children needed to be with their mother.

However, to provide his family's wants as well as its needs, the man couldn't be at home very much. There wasn't time to teach Sunday School, so mother took over and little boys lost masculine leadership in religion. There wasn't time for fathers to practice ball, hunt, fish, or hike with their sons, so the sons didn't have the opportunity to develop respect for their fathers or for manhood. Many men started hiring odd jobs done around the house, so their sons also missed out on valuable work training from their fathers. These undeveloped sons grew up to be the fathers of today and have, for the most part, perpetuated the lack of developing a strong father-son relationship. It is no surprise that sons and fathers feel alienated from each other. Boys now seek fellowship and even leadership from other boys or their hero images and, therefore, develop into insecure male adults.

Daughters have also been deeply scarred by the father's removal from the family. Girls during the 50's grew up on "Father Knows Best" and other programs that pictured ideal fathers who firmly, but kindly, led the family fairly and lovingly. These ideal fathers were home evenings and weekends and could always be depended on to listen, care, and even demonstrate their love with a hug and a kiss. How unlike most real fathers then and since. When these fathers were home, they were exhausted physically or too emotionally drained to give anything.

So it has gone through the 70's and 80's. One untrained generation passed after another until now, approaching the end of the third generation, we are given a new opportunity. The parents of the home schooling movement are a hope for the future — a hope that families will be restored and strengthened by God's Word.

My prayer is that fathers will see the need for their leadership in the family — to train their children's behavior so that they will accept their mother's teaching; that mothers will back away from any attempt to run the family and will ask their husbands for guidance; that fathers will give proper love and affection to their daughters, especially during their early teen years; and that fathers will spend time with their sons in becoming men together. Through work, recreation, and

Christian service, a father and his son can be drawn together - the father gaining insight and understanding and the son gaining respect and wisdom.

It all depends on you, Mr. Home School Father. Will you be one of the "few good men" of this generation?

SECTION III

PRACTICAL SUGGESTIONS

This section contains some practical suggestions on getting started successfully with your home schooling adventure. It also provides some excellent suggestions on selecting your curriculum and some final words of encouragement.

Steps in Starting a Home School

1.   Father and mother *both* need to discuss the prospect of home schooling – why they believe it should be done and the sacrifice that each must make in order to accomplish the task.

a. Speak together to other experienced home school families about the benefits and pitfalls.

b. Read books like *The Peanut Butter Family* and articles in *The Teaching Home* by successful home schooling families to envision the value of success. (While most men don't care much for studying on top of their job requirements, a wife can offer to read a chapter or so each evening out loud and then they could discuss what was read.)

2.   Father and mother *both* need to read and discuss the contents of this booklet and at least one each of the recommended books on humanism, legal issues, and child training. This study will help to develop a deep conviction about home schooling instead of just a simple emotional desire.

3.   Attending a local support group's meetings for a couple of months will also help build convictions as will getting to know other home schooling families.

4.   Once the decision is made to home school, there are several steps to take in preparation.

a. Check with your local support group or state association about the attitude of your public officials toward home schooling. Consider joining Home School Legal Defense Association.

b. Don't make a scene when you pull your child out of public school! Nothing will raise the ire and righteous indignation of school officials more than for their perceived authority to be challenged. If close to a semester's end, wait until then to withdraw.

If the laws in your state allow home schooling, and you are

able by conscience to conform with them, simply request that all of your children's academic records be transferred to you.

If you are unable to conform to state laws, it might be best to enroll your children in a correspondence or satellite school that could then request transfer of their records. Otherwise, I recommend that you go to the officials who administer the law (school or state) and respectfully request an exemption on the basis of what information (if any) you believe is right to provide them. Example: The state law may say you are required to be a state certified teacher. You, on the other hand, believe that God holds "little ole uncertifiable you" responsible for teaching your own children. However, you may be willing (as per Romans 13:1-4) to offer to take the state teachers' competency test to prove you meet minimal standards. (Any adult should be able to pass this approximately 8th grade test.)

If the officials deny your reasonable offer, and you are prepared to serve God rather than man, make sure your HSLDA fees are paid up in advance and be prepared for the legal battle to come before quietly removing your children from school. *Caution:* protect your testimony through quality home schooling, as unto the Lord. If home schooling laws in your state are not favorable and you are not willing to make an open, but respectful stand to get them changed, the Biblical solution is to move to another state which has laws more favorable to home schooling.

c. Request, in writing, the transfer of your child's records from the public or Christian school. Many parents even give a name to their home school and some incorporate them before asking for records. Naming and/or incorporating your school all depends on your state's laws, ordinances, and even your local school superintendent's attitude.

d. Join *Home School Legal Defense Association* before you have any encounter with officials. The $100 you pay per year for your entire family not only obtains an extremely knowledgeable advocate when needed, it gives you a great peace of mind and helps to fight for parents' God-given rights nation-wide. Even families in states where home schooling is perfectly legal have been harassed by local officials. No one is immune from harassment.

e. If you haven't already, join your state home school association, a local support group, and subscribe to the *Teaching Home* magazine.

4. Finally, select your curriculum. Home school families new and old, make too much of a problem out of this decision. There is no *one* right curriculum for your child. At best curriculum is a tool, at worst it can be a slave master. Remember, *you* are now in charge of your child's education. Grade levels, starting or ending dates for school, number of hours per day, course of study for each grade are all inventions of the public school system designed for *mass* education without consideration for the individual.

If you obtained proper test results on your child, you know as much or more about where he is and what he should be able to handle as any teacher before you. It doesn't matter if your child has to go back two grade levels or is able to jump ahead one. The objective is learning, not advancement with the masses. When your child is properly placed where he belongs in any curriculum, real education can begin. He can then comprehend the content and pass the tests thereby building self confidence and even developing self motivation. As a result your job as the teacher will be a joy instead of the nightmare it would have been trying to drag a child through material beyond his ability.

With these things in mind you are ready to select a curriculum. Remember, curriculum is only a tool and any curriculum can be used by a dedicated teacher (you) to obtain positive results. However, each curriculum has certain distinctives of which home school parents should be aware. The next article overviews those distinctions.

For a more complete coverage of getting started issues, read:

The Christian Home School
    Gregg Harris
The Big Book of Home Learning (4 vol.)
    Mary Pride
A Survivors Guide to Home Schooling
    Shackelford & White

Selecting A Curriculum
by David J. Korecki

When it comes to choosing a curriculum, what considerations should a parent make? It takes only a brief survey into the area of home schooling to realize that there is a bewildering array of ideas on how, when, and what a child ought to be taught. At first, choosing a curriculum may seem too difficult, but it is not as complicated as it may seem. However, a good choice is not made by simply reviewing a comparison chart of all curricula. The answer to which curriculum is best can be best obtained through a series of varied considerations.

The Multitude of Choices

Secular Versus Christian - Does it matter?

Absolutely! One of the greatest blessings to the cause of home education has been the development of Christian curriculum. No longer do Christian parents have to wade through pages of secular texts on the lookout for values and ideals that conflict with their own. (In some cases Christian publishers have not written texts for everything a home schooler may wish to teach his children. For instance, when it comes to state histories, a parent will still be forced to utilize secular texts and must exercise discernment and guidance in their use. But these areas are few). A child's views should be shaped by God's perspective of life, something secular texts fail to do. Instead, with the aid of a Christian curriculum parents should be able to work in conjunction with the church for the total development of their children.

Acceptability -The curriculum of choice should reflect the values that are desired to be taught to children. Rather than undermining the authority of God, parents, church, or government; curriculum should reinforce a family's values. The false concepts of innate goodness of man, situation ethics, and values clarification; do not need to be spoon-fed to children underneath their parents' noses. Secular humanism, the denial of the existence of heaven and hell, or failure to show the need for man's immortal souls to be saved from sin, will only give a warped view of reality. A Christian curriculum is a must! The apostle Paul put it this way, "Beware lest any man spoil you through philosophy and vain deceit, after the tradition of men, after the rudiments of the world, and not after Christ." (Colossians 2:8).

There is no need to worry about sacrificing quality either. By and large Christian curricula follow the same subjects and sequence that secular texts follow, but are written from a Biblical perspective. In fact in many instances the Christian curricula exceeds the academic quality of the secular texts.

Accreditation - Curriculum publishers of public school textbooks such as Harcourt Brace Jovanovich, MacMillan Publishing Co. or publishers for Christian textbooks like Bob Jones University Press or Alpha Omega Publications are not accredited. It is the schools which seek accreditation not the curriculum publishers. However, some state and most local school boards approve the book lists from which their schools can buy.

The bottom line is that parents do not generally *need* to use secular texts. Without a doubt it is far better to utilize a curriculum that is thoroughly Christian.

Type Of Home School- It may determine your curriculum.

Correspondence School - There are a number of complete home school programs available. They include all the necessary curriculum and lesson plans (some even have audio or video tapes). The only choice in curriculum is in which correspondence school to enroll. Lessons are sent to and graded by the school. Grades, report cards, and transcripts are provided by the school. Time limits are usually recommended for the student to encourage completion within a reasonable length of time.

Satellite School - Sometimes this is called a home extension or umbrella program. This is for the family that wants help with standardized testing, a place to turn for counsel, record keeping, or resource personnel. You still maintain control and responsibility for what takes place in your home school, but assistance with parent training, attendance records, and credibility is provided by the umbrella organization. Local churches, Christian schools, or home schooling guidance centers will often let home schoolers set up underneath their care. Belonging to such an association may or may not allow you to freely choose all of your curriculum. The extent of the control exerted on the home school varies and should be determined before enrolling.

Support group affiliate - Often several home school families will get together to help each other in the home education process. The group may purchase curriculum in bulk in order to save money thereby restricting curriculum choices somewhat. They may ask an art teacher to come in once a week to teach the children of several families or allow another person to teach children in subjects where those children's parents feel inadequate. It can also be a place to exchange ideas and resources that may be the encouragment that's needed for the day.

Independent Home School-Many parents want no restrictions on what they do. They are full of ideas and anxious to train their children. An independent home school demands more of the individual parent than being enrolled in some sort of program. In this case the choice of curriculum is *entirely* up to the parent as is the responsibility for making a good choice.

Multigrade Teaching - What factors make a difference?

Number of Children - The family with only one child has a considerably easier job than the family that must teach in a multilevel situation. Textbooks are wonderful to use if there is only one child, or two or more children can be taught the same thing together. However, trying to teach two or more children at different levels out of the same book is quite a challenge for the beginner. One of the most important factors to consider in teaching more than one child at home is the amount of time it will take on the parents' part. Preparing multiple lesson plans for various courses and for several children can be very time consuming. These families should perhaps consider the advantage of a curriculum that is geared for personalized teaching or has a multilevel management system.

Children's Ages - Each child is different and depending on the age of a child, presentation can make a big difference. Easy to handle curriculum with easy-to-read text is essential when the children are young. Younger children will enjoy the use of either the textbook and workbooks or worktexts. However, younger children have difficulties moving back and forth from a text to a workbook with their eyes and their attention. The older the children are, the more likely it is that parents will need help when subjects are taught in which the parents have not studied for years or not at all. In these situations teaching aids become very helpful, whether they are included as part of the students materials, as in a worktext, or as part of a teacher manual or handbook.

Note: There is a big controversy over the correct age to begin teaching children formally – like to read and to be accountable for remembering what is taught. Please read Mr. Fugate's booklet, *"Will Early Education Ruin Your Child?"* This book deals with both extremes in the philosophy of early education – those of creating super babies and delayed instruction. The only correct philosophy must be based on Scripture and be consistent with true science and logic. This book finally resolves this issue for any Christian parents' peace of mind. It deals with early vs. late, formal vs. informal, play vs. work, and other educational issues.

Parents' ability and time - The confines of time and space take a noticeable toll on the parent. Choose a curriculum that takes into consideration just how much personal ability, time, and space you have available. Adjusting to a curriculum that mom or dad has a hard time keeping up with can be a terrible strain on the family. Choose a curriculum that fits both the parent as well as the student.

Down To the Basics - Does the format of curriculum matter?

Format means the physical characteristics of a curriculum's presentation. There are basically two formats from which to choose or you can create your own format. Each is distinct in some way from the others.

Textbooks - are a literary presentation of the principles of a subject. They are designed to be an organized resource of information on a subject. They may be hardbound or softbound and they may include, in addition to the textbook itself, student workbooks or worksheet materials. They require the parent to be the teacher in the same fashion as in a traditional classroom. It is up to the parent to adapt the material's presentation to suit the needs of individual students. The textbook itself offers no insight into the child's progress or lack of it. Insight is gained by measuring a student's progress with lesson plan objectives, separate tests, and quizzes. The beauty of textbooks is found in their being a comprehensive overview of a subject and their exclusion of any personalized work space. Textbooks can therefore be readily reused.

Worktexts - are a combination of textbook and workbook in one unit. Tests, quizzes, and activities are all a part of the same physical book. Worktexts fall into two categories: Self-instructional and Tutorial. Self-instructional worktexts are designed for programmed learning where the curriculum plays the total role of the teacher. Students must attain a certain skill level or proficiency in a given subject before progressing.

The tutorial worktexts on the other hand, are flexible. They allow various degrees of interaction between teacher and student. Work is presented in such a way as to allow the parent to function as a teacher, tutor, or monitor. Worktexts are flexible enough to allow students to progress according to their own ability while establishing more accountability to the teacher. The student in either case can experience progress and receive encouragement with the successful completion of each small unit.

Create your own format- This is a child-directed approach to learning that emphasizes the child's areas of interest. Referred to sometimes as *package studies* or *unit studies*, these self contained units provide instruction through a variety of means. The purpose of these units, whether prepackaged or made by home school parents, is to motivate a student through his own interests. There are no restrictions as to what goes into the package except those the manufacturer or parent establishes. Since there is no prescribed format, it is difficult to predict what the end results will be as well as almost impossible to measure objectively. Results will vary from package to package and from student to student. This format is not recommended for the novice home school parent.

Complete Curriculum Or Smorgasbord - Which is best?

A complete curriculum is one that has either all subjects or at least a single discipline laid out in planned sequence. The smorgasbord approach is a common phenomena among veteran home schoolers. In it, parents create their own curriculum for their children by picking and choosing what they feel to be the best from all of the various curricula and other resources. While some veteran home schoolers have the expertise to do this, it is probably not the wisest choice for the beginner. There are at least four factors that will help put the decision into clearer focus, and show why a complete curriculum is a better way to begin in home schooling.

Scope and Sequence - A complete curriculum is created around a comprehensive guide of the content and order of materials for each subject at each level. In simple terms, it indicates not only what, but also when everything ought to be taught. Its purpose is to ensure that everything necessary to be covered is covered and that it is presented at the appropriate place. If the beginning home schooler chooses to follow this course of study, he can be assured that the material is presented in a way to maximize learning through a systematic progression. If parents do not utilize a complete curriculum, they must know the scope and sequence of each curriculum they wish to use in their collage.

Integration - Not too many years ago, secular publishers sought to integrate the various academic disciplines. This means that when studying math, a student would also encounter material that related to the study of English or science. In the smorgasbord approach to curriculum, this is often tried by home schoolers. Care must be taken to be certain that the reading level of the material being integrated is not above the reading ability of the child. Frequently the integration has proven to be more of a hindrance than a help to a student, confusing rather than clarifying the material. First year home schoolers need not concern themselves with integration.

Learning Gaps - This is a very serious problem that can result from the smorgasbord approach. Unfortunately the only way to recognize it is after the fact. Learning gaps are holes in a students academic attainment. Unless a parent is constantly evaluating curriculum and slotting various books for review to be sure no breaks occur, learning gaps will result.

Student Placement - Diagnostic testing - Another problem is knowing exactly where to place a student in relation to his abilities and attainment. Your options are to place them at their grade level according to age, or take a guess at where in the curriculum they should start. By far the best option is to use diagnostic placement tests that allow you to place a child in a complete curriculum at exactly the point that he belongs.

Beginning home schoolers will save themselves much time, work, and anguish by choosing a complete curriculum rather than the smorgasbord approach.

Teacher Helps, Lesson Plans, Teacher Handbooks
Do you need them?

The answer to this question depends on your needs. Many of these items are not necessary to be successful in teaching your own children. Before you decide *not* to buy them however, take a close look at what they may offer to the beginning home school. Teacher handbooks can provide detailed descriptions of how to progress through a curriculum, organize instructional units, provide supplemental instruction information, provide lists of resources, give you hints and tips on how to present a lesson, or give suggestions on supplemental activities. They may also include the answers to worksheets, quizzes, and tests. Unless you have the time to work through every question yourself, this feature alone could be worth the price of the handbook or teachers manual. The decision to purchase teacher-helps really boils down to whether or not there is a need for organizational aids, an additional teaching resource, or answers to curriculum questions.

Not every home school needs these extras. Count the cost to your own time, peace of mind, and pocketbook before you blindly purchase all those teacher aids. Some of these supposed time savers actually take longer to use than they are worth. Prices can range from five to fifty dollars per subject. A parent with a good head on his shoulders might try to do without some of them. Be careful though, if the aids are integral to the successful teaching of a curriculum, get them. Remember, monetary and time investment in proper teacher resources usually results in a better prepared and more capable teacher.

It is recommended that you ask others who have used the specific curriculum that you are considering. Ask them if they found the helps necessary and why or why not. If the publisher has material explaining the use of their helps, read it and determine if they would be of personal benefit to you. Beginning home schoolers should seriously consider every help available.

Finances - What do you want to spend?

A chief concern to any parent is finances. By electing home schooling over public education, parents are incurring an additional expense. At the same time by electing to home school rather than sending their children to a Christian school they are going to spend considerably less. The option of home schooling is relatively inexpensive financially. What you actually spend will be dependent on what basic curriculum format you choose.

Textbooks - Textbooks have been king in education for years. This is the one format with which most parents are familiar. Each parents' own education was filled with textbooks. Textbooks can average about twenty-five dollars apiece. Yes, they do cost more than worktexts or coming up with your own material, but they can be resold. Also used books can be passed down to younger children or be circulated among home school families. After all, textbooks are made to last from three to five years. Their cost usually runs one and a half to two times as much as consumable worktexts. Complete cost per year per student ranges from two hundred to four hundred dollars including all teacher aids.

Worktexts - The financial beauty of worktexts is that they may generally be bought one at a time, and in any order you want. If money is short, you can purchase only what you need to get by for the next month or two. No large up front investment is necessary to begin as with textbooks. Worktexts also tend to save on supplies such as loose-leaf notebooks and paper. A complete year of curriculum for one student ranges from one hundred to one hundred fifty dollars including all teacher aids.

Correspondence school - Remember when enrolling students in a correspondence school that you are buying more than curriculum. Support and credibility are the prime enticements for enrolling and also the reason for additional expenses over purchasing just curriculum. The service of a legal umbrella, record keeping, grading, a ready source of counsel, and other such things may be worth the additional money. The costs vary from one hundred fifty dollars to four hundred dollars per child.

Satellite School- Belonging to a satellite school normally does not cost a great deal. It all depends on the supplies and services offered. Usually only small fees are charged for these services but the inclusion of curriculum would significantly change the cost.

Questions of Competency

Choosing Curriculum - It's only a servant.

The one thing that should result from reading this chapter is to have your mind set at ease concerning the difficulty of choosing curriculum. There is no perfect curriculum. Any conscientious parent should be able to evaluate curriculum by making the decisions discussed in the preceeding section. Remember, curriculum is only a tool to be used by the hand of a parent as the teacher. You are still in charge of the curriculum. If something about it causes concern, do something about it. You can always double check the facts or be innovative with your own proven ideas and techniques.

One of the most frequent sources of frustration for the beginning home schooler, is trying to decide which curriculum is best. Secular educators and sometimes, sad to say, even Christian educators insist that a parent, unless trained specifically in education, is inept when it comes to teaching their children. Worse than this however, is the docile submission of parents to the dogged attacks on their competency as educators. Not only have parents been teaching their children at home for years, they have also determined the scope and sequence of their children's education until they were sent to formal school. Parents are also able, with some study, to select proper curriculum for their children's academic education.

Know Your Children And Their Needs

There is not another person alive who has more opportunity to know their children than parents themselves. Day in and day out, children live with mom and dad. Being on the firing line with the children, a parent knows what gets their attention and what does not. The choice of curriculum should not only be academically acceptable but also suited to the individuality of each child.

Discern Counsel From Other Home Schoolers

While many people will look upon parents with horror at the thought of considering home schooling their own children, other home schoolers will not. In fact they will be more than willing to advise you on everything from scheduling to choosing curriculum. One caution, however, other home schoolers will be biased. Be sure to look beyond the things they recommend and find out *why* they recommend them. Consider the number and age range of children. Does the mother have a similar organizational ability, drive, mental alertness. How successful have these parents been with home schooling? Do they have their children under control? Considerations like these will help in formulating a decision. Think through the advice of other home schoolers. Remember what works for one family, may or may not work for another.

Complete a Full Year With Your Curriculum Choice.

As stated before, there is no perfect curriculum. But there are no perfect parents either. After a decision has been made and the school year begins, stick it out. Make a commitment to that core curriculum. This stability will minimize confusion and frustration to the students and parents. The first several months of any curriculum and, indeed, home schooling itself are going to be difficult enough to adjust to. Let this year be a time for parents, as well as students, to learn. Sticking with curriculum will help identify goals, methods, and structure that are desirable or undesirable. Then parents can determine what they ultimately want in a curriculum. Before long they, in turn, will be advising other families about curriculum choices. You may wish to read Mary Pride's *Big Book of Home Learning (4 Vol.)*, and then attend your local support group's or state association's curriculum fair to see what is availble for yourself.

You Can Do It!

Although home schooling is a challenge, many families are blessed abundantly by the experience. Everyone is at least a little lazy and self-centered and home schooling is work requiring self-sacrifice. We would have to admit that no one would take on this project unless they love their children and want the very best for them. But if you will step out in faith, you will find that God can provide all of the power you need to be successful in home schooling.

I've known families in which the marriage was improved and even healed through working together on this endeavor. I've heard of many children who have been led to Christ by their own parents while studying Christian curriculum and of hundreds of children growing up with respect and honor toward their parents. I've spoken to thousands of Christians from widely varied churches who come together in fellowship and unity around this extremely important issue. God is certainly empowering and blessing the home school movement and the individual families taking part.

The biggest obstacle the average family today must overcome in order to home school, is that of the working mother. There are two types of working mothers (not counting the single mother who has no choice). The first is the dedicated career woman and the second is the woman who simply works to augment her husband's income. We will look at each of these separately. The Christian career woman should realize that she chose marriage. Now, since motherhood has come along, she needs to realize that she also chose family over her career. In other words, the Christian wife and mother has no legitimate option of a career outside of the family (unless she is required to work by her husband). She has already chosen two God-ordained callings.

Likewise, the husband of a working mother should reevaluate the value of her working, compared with her being allowed to function in her role of wife and mother. Many husband and wife teams find, upon careful examination, that the wife's net income (after all work-associated expenses have been deducted) is only 10% to 25% of her total salary. These expenses include income taxes, social security tax, child care or private school, housecleaning, laundry and extra dry cleaning, extra clothing for everyone, special working clothes for the wife, transportation, convenience foods and eating out. These items will normally run between $600 to $1200 per month. Thus, the average working mother who earns between $800 to $1500 probably only clears $200 to $300 per month. This is an amount that a family business might be able to produce while teaching the children about work at the same time. Many home school families have even discovered that decreasing their standard of living to an amount within the husband's income was possible.

Working women need to be aware that the world may have enticed them with the lust for possessions, pride of self-importance, and the constant stimulation of other people and activity. For some mothers it is a sacrifice of Godly proportions to give up their work and return home. Especially if they believe that only boredom, drudgery, and lack of personal challenge awaits them there. If they only knew how much creativity and intellect it takes to run a well-ordered home and home school, they might look forward to their new challenge. Surely, they would come home with a better attitude if they understood the blessings God has in store for the dedicated wife and mother.

I believe that a home school is best run like a farm or a business where each one has his or her own duties. This is especially true when there are several children. A typical break-down of duties might go like this:

Father — Principal

1. Establishes obedience standards and follows up when children break his standards or reject the authority of the mother.

2. Evaluates all testing results and sets up a course of action (i.e., grade level, how much progress is expected by the student for the year, month, week).

3. Establishes household duties for each child (rooms clean, beds made, breakfast prepared, clean-up schedule, garbage take out, and any others).

4. Teaches devotions (at least once weekly).

5. Follows up weekly with each child privately and individually during a walk, a ride, or some other activity. This habit will give dad an opportunity to ask what was learned that week and then to *listen*..

NOTE: Some fathers will not be willing to invest their time in home schooling the first year, but will support their committed wife's efforts. Such a situation can work, but the wife needs to be alert that her home schooling efforts don't rob too much time or attention from her husband. Perhaps he will take an active part after a year or two, especially if the wife asks his opinion on schedules, devotions, career planning, and enforcement of standards.

Mother — Teacher/Administrator

1. Handles all teaching, ordering of materials, and record keeping. Selects curriculum in keeping with her natural abilities and maintains progress as agreed upon with the father. Reports progress or lack thereof to the father.

2. Upholds father's preset standards as well as the other instructions she gives the children. Disciplines for any infractions of *her* rules, and reports infractions of those of the father's to him.

3. Makes sure she retains some private time for herself to lie down, shop, visit, read, or some other way to relax. A good way to start would be to take one hour per day and one afternoon per week for herself.

Children — Learners/Helpers

1. Apply themselves diligently to their studies. Help brothers and sisters as they are able.

2. Fulfill all duties as unto the Lord. Look for other ways to help parents with work load.

Most families today have never operated with a schedule and assignments, but will find them essential for successful home schooling. Remember, you are learning and maturing right along with your children.

There is no other teacher to compare with the parent who is willing to commit to the education of his or her child. Parents are more likely to be successful teachers because they possess the authority and rightful power to bring their child under control so that true learning can then occur. Only a parent can give one-on-one tutoring commensurate with each child's natural abilities. Even a parent who lacks education can learn ahead of, or along with, her child. A state certified teacher who had become a home school mother once told me,

> Tell all the mothers that having a degree in education wouldn't help. I had to unlearn almost everything I had been taught in order to teach my own children. The average common-sense homemaker is better off.

No one knows your child better than you do — his needs, character flaws, and potential. Who could do a better job than you? Let me encourage you as one who has been there, *you can do it!*

APPENDICES

Appendix A
Key Addresses

Home School Legal Defense Association
Paeonian Springs, VA   22129
(703) 882-3838

Teaching Home (Bi-monthly Magazine)
12311 NE Brazee
Portland, OR   97230
(503) 253-9633

Home Sweet Home (Quarterly Newsletter)
P.O. Box 1254
Milton, WA   98354
(206) 922-5941
Mark and Laurie Sleeper

Home School Research (Newsletter & Reports)
School of Education
Seattle Pacific University
Seattle, WA 98119
(206) 281-2360
Brian Ray, Ph. D.

Christian Life Workshop
180 S.E. Kane Rd.
Gresham, OR   94080
(503) 667-3942
Gregg Harris

State Christian Home School Associations

These contacts can supply names of support groups near you and dates of curriculum fairs in the state.

Alabama. Alabama Home Educators, Box 160091, Mobile 36616.

Alaska. AK Private & Home Educators Assoc., Box 70, Talkeetna 99676.

Arizona. Christian Home Educators of Arizona, 3015 S. Evergreen Rd., Tempe 85282, (602)897-7688.

Arkansas. Arkansas Christian Home Education Assoc., Box 501, Little Rock 72203, (501)834-7729.

California. Christian Home Educators Assoc., Box 28644, Santa Ana 92799, (714)537-5121.

Colorado. Homes Offering Meaningful Education, 1015 S. Gaylord St., #226 Denver 80209, (303)567 4800.

Connecticut. The Education Assoc. of Christian Homeschoolers, Box 446, Broad Brook 06106.

Delaware. Tri-State Home School network, Box 7193, newark 19714.

Florida. Florida at Home, 7615 Clubhouse Estates Dr., Orlando 32819.

Georgia. Georgians for Freedom in Education, 5986 Randy Lane, Ellenwood GA 30049, (404)961-8416.

Hawaii. Christian Homeschoolers of Hawaii, 91-824 Oama St., Ewa Beach 96706, (808)689-6398.

Idaho. Idaho Home Educators, Box 4022, Boise 83711.

Illinois. Illinois Christian Home Educatiors, Box 261, Zion 60099.

Indiana. IN Assoc. of Home Educators, Box 17135, Indianapolis 46217.

Iowa. Iowa Home Educators Assoc. Box 213, Des Moines 50301.

Kansas. Teaching Parents Assoc. 100 E. 109th St. N., Valley Center 67147 (316)755 2159.

Kentucky. Kentucky Christian Home School Assoc., 1301 Bridget, Fairdale 40118, (502)363-5104.

Louisiana. Christian Home Educators Fellowship of LA, Box 14421, Baton Rouge 70898, (504)642-2059.

Maine. ME Homeschool Assoc., Box 3283, Auburn 04210, 777-1700.

Maryland. Maryland Assoc. of Christian Home Eduation Organ., Box 1041, Emmitsburg 21727, (301)662-0022.

Massachusetts. MA Home Schooling Organization of Parent Educators, 15 Ohio St., Wilmington 01887, (508)658-8970.

Michigan. Informatin Network for Christian Homes, 4150 Ambrose NE, Grand Rapids 49505, (616)364-4438.

Minnesota. MN Assoc. of Christian Home Educators, Box 188, Anoka 55303, 753-2370

Mississippi. Mississippi Home Educators Associatin, Box 2067, Starkville 39759, (601)324-2668.

Missouri. Families for Home Education, 21709 E. Old Atherton Rd., Independence 64058, (816)796-0978.

Montana. Homeschoolers of MT, Box 40 Billings MT 59104, (406)248-6762.

Nebraska. Nebraska Home Education Assoc., 5000 Grand View Ln., Lincoon 68521, (402)476-9925.

Nevada. Nevada Home Schools, Box 21323, Reno 89515.

New Hampshire. Christian Home Educators of NH, Box 1653, Hilsboro 03244.

New Jersey. Education Network of Christian Home-schoolers, 65 middlesex Rd. Matawan 07747, 583-7128

New Mexico. New Mexico Christian Home Educators, 5749 Pardise Blvd. NW, Albuquerque 87114, 897-1772.

New York. Loving Education At Home, Box 332, Syracuse 13205, (518)377-6019.

North Carolina. North Carolinians for Home Education, 204 N. Person St. Raleigh 27601, (919)834-6243.

North Dakota. North Dakot Home School Assoc., Box 539, Turtle Lake 58575, (701)448-9193.

Ohio. Christian Home Educators of OH, Box 1224, Kent 44240, 673-7272.

Oklahoma. Coalition of Chr. Home Educators of OK, Box 471032, Tulsa 74147.

Oregon. Oregon Christian (home) Education Assoc. Network, 2515 NE 37th Porlland 97212, 288-1285.

Pennsylvania. Parent Educators of Pennsylvania, RD 2, Box 141, Wrightsville 17368. (717)252-0286.

Rhode Island. RI Guild of Home Teachers, 272 Pequot Ave., Warwick 02886, (401)737-2265.

South Carolina. SC Home Educatos Assoc., Box 33, Goose Creek 29445.

South Dakota. W. Dakota Christian Home Schools, Box 528, Black Hawk 5778.

Tennessee. TN Home Educatin Assoc., 3677 Richbriar Ct., Nashville 37211, (615)834-3529.

Texas. Home-Oriented Private Education for TX, Box 43887, Austin 78745-0018, (512)280-HOPE.

Utah. Utah Christian Home Schooling, 3190 S. 4140 W., W. Valley City 84120.

Vermont. Vermont Home Schoolers Assoc., Spruce Knob Rd., Middleton 05757, (802)235-2103.

Virginia. Home Educators Assoc. of Virginia, Box 1810, Front Royal 22630, (703)635-9322,.

Washington. WA Assoc. of Teaching Chr. Homes, Box 554, Colville 99114.

West Virginia. WV Home Education Assoc., Box 266, Glenville 26351, 462-8296.

Wisconsin. WI Parents Assoc., Box 2502, Madison 53701.

Wyoming. Homeschoolers of WY, Box 2197, Mills 82644, 235-4928.

Appendix B
Recommended Reading List

A Survivor's Guide to Home Schooling – Shackelford/White
Crossway Books
A Division of Good News Publishers
9825 West Roosevelt Road
Westchester, IL 60154

Big Book of Home Learning (The) – Pride
Crossway Books
A Division of Good News Publishers
9825 West Roosevelt Road
Westchester, IL 60154

Battle For The Mind (The) – LaHaye
Fleming H. Revell
184 Central Ave.
Old Tappan, NJ 07675

Child Abuse In the Classroom – Schlaffly
Eagle Forum
P. O. Box 618
Alton, IL 62002

Christian Home School (The) – Harris
Wolgemuth & Hyatt Publishers, Inc.
P.O. Box 1941
Brentwood, TN 37027

Is It Ever Too Early – Claggett
Dove Christian Publications
1425 Aurora Road
Melbourne, FL 32935
(407) 242-8290

Peanut Butter Family (The) – Butterworth
Fleming H. Revell
184 Central Ave.
Old Tappan, NJ 07675

Sidetracked Home Executives – Young/Jones
Warner Books
666 5th Avenue
New York, NY 10103

Should Home Schoolers Obey the Law? – Farris
Home School Legal Defense Association
Paeonian Springs, VA 22129

Successful Home Schooling – Fugate
Aletheia Division
Alpha Omega Publications
P.O. Box 3153
Tempe, AZ   85280
(800)622-3070

Telling Yourself the Truth – Backus/Chapian
Bethany House Publishers
6820 Auto Club Road
Minneapolism, MN 55438

What Are They Teaching Our Children? – Gabler
Educational Research Analysts
P. O. Box 7518
Longview, TX 75607-7518

What The Bible Says About Child Training – Fugate
Aletheia Division
Alpha Omega Publications
P.O. Box 3153
Tempe, AZ   85280
(800)622-3070

Who Owns the Children? – Adams/Blair
Truth Forum
P. O. Box 18929
Austin, TX 78760

Will Early Education Ruin Your Child? – Fugate
Aletheia Division
Alpha Omega Publications
P.O. Box 3153
Tempe, AZ   85280
(800)622-3070

Appendix C
HOME SCHOOL LEGAL DEFENSE ASSOCIATION

"And you shall love the Lord your God with all your heart and with all your soul and with all your might. And these words, which I am commanding you today, shall be on your heart; and you shall teach them diligently to your [children] and shall talk of them when you sit in your house and when you walk by the way and when you lie down and when you rise up."
Deuteronomy 6:5-7 *NASB*

"The Child is not the mere creature of the state; those who nurture him and direct his destiny have the right, coupled with the high duty, to recognize and prepare him for additional obligations."
United States Supreme Court, Pierce v. Society of Sisters, 268 U.S. 510, 1925

Purpose

Home schooling is an idea whose time has come — again. Parents are once again assuming their God-given duty and privilege of teaching their children at home.

Many families are finding that their children do better academically, socially, and spiritually when they are taught in their home environment by loving and dedicated parents.

One of the persistent roadblocks to many parents is the question of the legality of home schooling. Indeed, many parents have faced criminal prosecution for teaching their children at home. Generally, only a few home schoolers in any community are selected for prosecution. When this happens, the family faces enormous legal expense, mostly for attorneys' fees.

Families who are not prosecuted are often intimidated into giving up or moving by the mere threat of prosecution.

The Home School Legal Defense Association brings together a large number of home schooling families to enable each family to have a low-cost method of obtaining quality legal defense if the need arises.

We believe that home schooling, when it is responsibly done, is legally protected by the Constitution of the United States in all 50 states. We have found that many state laws are misinterpreted by school authorities, and often home schooling can continue after the authorities are shown the true meaning of local law.

The purpose of the Home School Legal Defense Association is to establish the fact that responsible home schooling is legally permissible in every state. We will provide experienced legal counsel and representation by qualified attorneys to every member family who is challenged in the area of home schooling. The attorneys' fees will be paid in full by the Association.

Your membership will help others to establish their right to home school in difficult states, while protecting your rights in your state as well.

Responsibility

We believe that God imposes a responsibility on all parents to train their children in a manner pleasing to Him and that this includes the ability to read and write well, to have a working knowledge of math, and to know and appreciate the history of our country.

We will accept for membership only those who are committed to honorably discharging their parental responsibilities.

The membership requirements set out in our application are for the sole purpose of enabling us to prove in court that families are responsibly fulfilling their duty to teach their children. We will not place restrictions on families. The membership criteria simply enable us effectively to defend each family in court if necessary.

Benefits of Membership

1. In the event that threatened or actual legal action is brought against a member family, the Association will furnish legal representation in any court proceeding at no additional charge beyond the membership fee. This service covers more than 80% of all defense costs in most cases. Member families will be responsible for additional defense costs, such as expert witness expenses, court costs, and deposition fees, which are beyond the actual time spent by an attorney retained by the Association. The Association's legal counsel is coordinated by Michael P. Farris, J. Michael Smith and Christopher J. Klicka.

2. After the matter has already gone through the first trial level, HSLDA will appeal members' cases to whatever higher courts are necessary to preserve the home schoolers' rights. However, HSLDA reserves the right to refuse to underwrite or approve an appeal. This right of refusal will only be exercised in the event the case, in HSLDA's opinion, presents "bad facts" that will set bad precedent endangering the right of other home schoolers.

3. We will provide a quarterly newsletter, *The Home School Court Report*, sent to member families at no extra charge, covering legal issues and other matters of concern to home schooling parents.

4. As resources permit, we will provide testimony at legislative hearings concerning home schooing matters.

Cost of Membership

The cost is $100 per year, per family. This is to be paid upon enrollment. It is to your advantage to apply during the month of June (or earlier) for an upcoming school year. The application process takes much longer during the months of July, August, and September. The Association reserves the right to refuse any membership application. If a family has received contact prior to their membership, approval normally will not be granted.

Savings

Although attorneys' fees will vary widely from state to state and situation to situation, the Association has estimated legal fees to give some idea of the typical costs involved.

Response to threats by local official . . . . . . $100 minimum
Initial Court hearings $1,000
Trial in Court of Record $5,000
Representation at Appellate level $3,000

Quotes

I am much afraid that the schools will prove the very gates of hell, unless they diligently labor in explaining the Holy Scriptures, and engraving them in the hearts of youth. I advise no one to place his child where the Scriptures do not reign paramount. —Martin Luther

The statist notion that governmental power should supersede parental authority in all cases because some parents abuse and neglect children is repugnant to American tradition." —Supreme Court of the United States

Quality education and parental choice should never be conflicting goals, and I am delighted to see our country making progress in promoting both goals, whether in public schools, private schools, or home schools, I applaud those parents who care enough to be personally involved in the education of their children. — Former President Ronald Reagan

Comments from HSLDA Members

Thank you so much for offering this service at such a reasonable rate. We feel so much more peaceful knowing we have godly lawyers on our side! —Nypomo, CA

I was impressed with your attitude and your real concern for our local problem. Thanks for representing us. —Monroe, MI

Thank you for your help and assurances. We feel shaky treading on new ground and it's comforting to talk with those who've been there and know the territory. —Chicago, IL

Once again we are grateful to you for providing invaluable legal services and encouragement to American families committed to taking full responsibility for rearing and educating their children. Our prayers for you will continue. —Albany, NY

We definitely want to renew our membership but pray that we won't have to use it. We really feel from our hearts that this money is well spent to support those who do have to use your services. — Hewitt, TX

Thank you for sticking up for the "little guys" who want to do God's will with their children. —Columbus, OH

We want to thank you for the prompt, kind, and helpful attitude HSLDA has displayed in our situation. It is good to know we have dedicated, qualified, and concerned people to go to bat for us. HSLDA helps make it easier for us parents to carry out our responsiblities and conviction we feel God has given us. —Inyokern, CA

We are glad to be a part of HSLDA and we'll do our part to encourage others to join too! —Bangor, ME

President and Founder of HSLDA

Michael P. Farris is the President and Founder of the Home School Legal Defense Association. He formed HSLDA in March of 1983 to provide legal assistance for home schooling parents facing litigation. Michael is an attorney experienced in many First Amendment and religious liberty cases. He has argued cases in the United States Supreme Court, numerous federal courts, and in five state supreme courts. He has authored the book **Home Schooling and the Law**, which is soon to be published by Crossway Books. Michael and his wife Vickie home school their five daughters and one son.

Vice President & HSLDA Board Member

J. Michael Smith is an attorney and member of the California Bar. He is a native of Arkansas and is a graduate of the University of Arkansas as well as the University of San Diego Law School. Michael has assisted many home school families, and has spoken at home school conferences and before state legislatures throughout the U.S. After being in private practice for 16 years, he is now employed full-time by HSLDA. He and his wife Elizabeth are home schooling their children.

Executive Director of HSLDA

Christopher J. Klicka is an attorney and member of the Virginia State Bar. He is a graduate of Grove City College, Pennsylvania, and the O.W. Coburn School of Law. He wrote a 250-page legal analysis of home schooling called *The Home School Reporter* for the Rutherford Institute and also authored and continues to update the *Home Schooling In The United States: A Statutory Analysis* for HSLDA, which describes the legal atmosphere of home schooling in each state. Chris has handled over a thousand legal conflicts involving home schools throughout the country. He and his wife Tracy are home schooling their child.

Board Member of HSLDA

Jim Carden is a husband, father, and businessman, in Fort Worth, Texas. He graduated from Baylor University with a B.A. in Psychology. Jim has testified in several home schooling cases on behalf of HSLDA members. He and his wife Jeanie are considered pioneers in the modern home schooling movement, having home schooled their three children for 14 years. The Carden children have never attended conventional schools.

Board Member of HSLDA

George Stroh is a business merger and acquisition consultant. He and his wife Linda are leaders in the Nebraska Home Educators Association and have been involved in the home school movement since 1983. George is also a Bible teacher at his church and a member of the Board of Directors of *Sound Words*, an international Christian radio ministry. The Strohs have two daughters, Tiffany, a senior at the University of Nebraska and Natasha, their 10-year-old home school student.

HOME SCHOOL LEGAL DEFENSE ASSOCIATION
PAEONIAN SPRINGS, VIRGINIA   22129
PHONE: (703)882-3838

Call or write for an application.

About the author — J. Richard Fugate

Mr. Fugate has been the President and Chief Executive Officer of Alpha Omega Publications, Inc., since 1982. He was Vice President of Finance and Business Manager of Accelerated Christian Education, Inc., 1973-1976. From 1975 until 1977 he was the owner and Principal of American Heritage Christian Academy. He was the founder and Director of the Foundation for Biblical Research, 1979-1982.

Since authoring *What the Bible Says About...Child Training*, (book, film series, and syllabus), he has been the speaker for many child training seminars at local churches. He has also been a speaker for the 1984 & 1988 National Christian Home School Conventions, many state home school conventions, and Alpha Omega Publications Administrator Conferences. His next booklet, *Will Early Education Ruin Your Child?*, is also available from Alpha Omega Publications and Christian bookstores.

Mr. Fugate has written many articles on child rearing, home schooling, and general education in the *Teaching Home, S.M.S. Publications, Ministries Today, Concerned Women of America* and *Positive Approach* magazines.

The following information is a collection of those articles as well as contributions from several other home school fathers.